Great in Eight

Joan Tabb M.A.

Eight Winning Strategies for Getting a
Job in Today's Competitive Market

© Copyright 2010 by Great in 8 Coaching

All rights reserved. No part of this book may be reproduced in any form without written permission of the copyright owners. All images in this book have been reproduced with the knowledge and prior consent of the artists concerned, and no responsibility is accepted by producer, publisher, or printer for any infringement of copyright or otherwise, arising from the contents of this publication. Every effort has been made to ensure that credits accurately comply with information supplied.

Book design: Lauren Smith Brand Communications
Illustrations: Peter Hoey

Author's Statement

I created Greatin8Coaching.com book series to capture, codify and present, in a very concise and accessible format, the innovative strategies needed to learn new skills in today's quickly moving environment. My goal is to apply this concise and interactive approach to timely topics in the hopes of hastening the process of making today's innovative ideas tomorrow's common knowledge.

Dedication

This book is dedicated to the job seekers I have worked with who have the courage and tenacity to get in there, compete and realize their career visions (though tempered with reality). And, a special dedication to those of you who are taking your first critical steps on your fast track to career success.

"Today's innovative ideas are tomorrow's common knowledge."

—ANONYMOUS

Table of Contents

Introduction 5

Who This Book is Intended For 5

Who This Book is Not Intended For 6

For Recent College Graduates 6

What Are the Pre-requisites?. 6

How to Best Use Greatin8 6

Contact with the Author and Job Seeking Community 7

Strategy #1: Your New FULL TIME JOB. 8

Strategy #2: How Did I Get Here? 16

Strategy #3: Your Career Story 22

Strategy #4: The Emotional Roller Coaster 28

Strategy #5: Rallying Your Personal Network. 36

Strategy #6: The Interview is YOUR Audition 46

Strategy #7: To Join or Not to Join—Professional Associations and Social Media 52

Strategy #8: Landing the Job 58

About Joan 64

Author Appreciation. 65

Notes 66

Introduction

Today's job seeker faces the most competitive market this country has seen in decades. Millions of people have lost their jobs, and by some measures, for every available job there are six people waiting to fill it.

I've worked with hundreds of job seekers in my career as a coach and trainer, and I've noticed certain best practices that separate great job seekers from the merely good ones. Great job seekers are the ones who know how to do things that hasten the job search process considerably, catapulting them to more rapid job acquisition.

Given the terrible unemployment situation we're facing in 2010, I decided that the best way to help as many job seekers as possible, as quickly as possible, was to get these practices into as many job seekers' hands as possible, fast. It's vital that people learn how to prepare themselves to be top performers not only in their own fields, but also in their efforts toward gaining employment.

The eight strategies outlined in this book will help you not only become a more effective and efficient job seeker, it will also help relieve the stress that comes with the territory, and boost your confidence as you go through the process.

Who Is This Book Intended For?

This book is for the job seeker who's ready to get out from behind the computer. It's not that there aren't plenty of good online resources; it's just that there are more productive ways to launch an effective job search. Using these eight strategies will put you ahead of the pack.

If you're already good at using all the online tools, this book will help you take off from there. The skills you need to get a great job today are not what they used to be. The bar has been raised, and you have to raise your game to match it. This book is a compendium of the strategies used by top job seekers who, by necessity, have gone from good to great in response to today's tough job market.

Who This Book Is Not Intended For

If you're not sure what you want to do in your work life—if you don't have a sharp resumé prepared and a good working knowledge of your industry—you need to find other resources to support you in your job search.

For Recent College Graduates

In sections of the book where you're asked to reflect on past work experiences, you should think of your college classes, projects, extracurricular activities and internships. Describe how your college achievements reflect skills such as teamwork, research skills, time management, communication skills, etc.

What Are the Prerequisites?

Before you even get started, you need to be prepared with all of the following:
- Knowledge of your industry/type of job you are seeking
- Basic professional skills and competencies in your field
- Resumé
- Ability to seek out appropriate job listings
- Internet access

How to Best Use Greatin8

Greatin8Coaching.com books are designed with the best of learning technology and web technology. It is designed to be QUICK, USEFUL, and PERSONALIZED, giving you the most up-to-date best

practices on a given topic. In each of the eight sections you'll find:
- An explanation of the strategy
- Case studies to make the strategy real and concrete
- Exercises to help you apply and personalize the information

After you read and apply these eight best job search strategies, you will have a **personalized job seeking workbook**, comprised of all of the exercises you've completed. It will help you carry out your job search efficiently and effectively, putting you ahead of the pack in securing a new position.

This book is designed as series of eight important sessions. Each chapter is meant to be used in order, starting at Strategy 1 and ending at Strategy 8. Working through the book from beginning to end will position you most effectively for a successful job search.

Contact with the Author and Job Seeking Community

I hope you find this book useful, and I'd love to hear from you and share your questions, comments, and ideas as a way of creating a community on the topic. I will personally answer your questions or find experts who can. I will also put your questions out to our job seeking community. Feel free to submit your ideas for the job search process as a way of growing our collective knowledge. Additionally, send me your success story and I will share them with our community of Greatin8 readers! I promise to publish all success stories and share them with others for inspiration and motivation.

Email me at: joan@Greatin8Coaching.com

"Whatever you think you can do or believe you can do, begin it. Action has magic, grace, and power in it."

—JOHANN GOETHE

STRATEGY #1

Your New FULL TIME JOB

Congratulations, you now have a new full time job. It's called Manager of Job Procurement, and your job duties consist of finding employment. Think about it. You probably had a job where you worked 40 hours a week, if not longer. You probably had an office to go to, tools to use, and a boss to report to. You had colleagues, meetings, projects, and deadlines. If you're a recent college graduate, you had a class schedule, homework assignments, term papers to write, and tests to take.

At work you had evaluations and at school you received grades. You were part of a structured system with expectations, accountability and feedback. Now it's up to you to create your own structure. Design a plan, then set a specific start date with regular hours and stick to it.

Your first assignment is to plan how you'll spend your time. Plan for a 40-hour work week. Include all the regular activities you can think of. This is a general plan, and as you go through the rest of this book you'll enter additional specific activities and projects. It's vital that you plan your days and impose structure and accountability for yourself.

Good job seekers talk about planning and scheduling, but let's face it; for most of us, this is easier said than done. We start out with lots of enthusiasm and focus, but within a few days we end up getting distracted after a couple of hours at best. By the end of the week, we've found a whole list of "must-do" activities that take the place of our job search.

'When you get right down to the root meaning of the word 'succeed', you find that it simply means to follow through."

—F.W. NICHOL

Anxiety and Fear: Jim

Laid off after seven years at a large high-tech corporation, Jim was granted three months of outplacement services, which left him with two big binders full of information and a list of new contacts. He also left with feelings of anxiety and fear.

Each morning he dutifully opened his computer and spent hours looking at job listing sites, sending cover letters and resumés, and connecting with friends online. That would typically take him up to lunch. In the afternoons, he switched gears and went to the local coffee shop with his laptop, once again surfing the net looking at job sites and responding to postings.

Jim was getting nowhere fast, and he knew it. He started calling recruiters and felt like he was sinking into a dark hole; the same dark hole where he was sending dozens of resumés!

Jim realized that there was such a thing as too much freedom. Back in his corporate days, the structure was more or less imposed. He had his management by objective (MBO) and knew what was needed to achieve success each day, week, and quarter.

Sadly, he was not given that same kind of structured MBO, consequence/reward system anymore. He realized he needed to be his own manager and create his new full time job of getting a job.

Great job seekers have a plan, and they stick to it. They really want to land a great job, and they stay focused and committed until they reach that goal. They know that looking for a job is its own full time job. They use professional coaches or find a job-seeking buddy to hold them to their plan. They do the laundry and buy the groceries after job-search hours are over so they can focus exclusively on their job search because they know that's what's going to land them a new job sooner rather than later.

Six ingredients of a successful job search

Great job seekers understand that it's a numbers game. You've got to plan and track every connection, lead, meeting, networking activity, and resumé submission. In my work as a job search coach and trainer, I've identified six common ingredients of a successful job search plan:

1. Complete *Greatin8: Job Skills* exercises
2. Number of phone calls
3. Number of emails
4. Number of resumés/cover letters submitted
5. Number of face-to-face informational/interview meetings, professional association meetings
6. Number of hours doing research
7. Number of hours for self maintenance (exercise, meals, socializing, grooming, shopping, etc.)

"Lost time is never found again."

—BEN FRANKLIN

Job Search Plan—Daily Planning Tool

	Monday	Tuesday	Wednesday	Thursday	Friday
Greatin8 Exercise Completion					
Phone Calls					
Emails					
Resumés Submitted					
Meetings Arranged					
Research Hours					
Self Maintenance					

Use the chart on the opposite page to plan your daily job-search activities. Make copies of this page so you'll have a fresh one ready to use each week. Use the blank rows at the bottom to add your own activity items.

Accountability is Key—A Job Search Buddy is Essential

Now that you're your own manager, you may need some assistance with sticking to the structure you've created for yourself. Most people need some kind of accountability to others. We often see this with exercise buddies. If you're like 90 percent of people you WILL need some kind of external accountability. It can be a hired career coach, a friend, a family member, someone you met in outplacement, someone from your employment network, etc. Make sure it's someone you trust and who understands the job search program you've built for yourself. This individual absolutely needs to be a positive force in your life. They need to agree to be an enthusiastic cheerleader. As a career coach, I ask my clients to email me every evening, five nights a week. This is a great way to keep them on track and accountable to a schedule, and at the end of the week they can see all of their activities, assess their progress, make adjustments, and plan for the following week. As the weeks go by and they work according to their plan, confidence builds as they see how their discipline and perseverance is paying off with more contacts, meetings, and outreach.

Out of control: Amy

Amy had been laid off for eight months. Her layoff came at an especially bad time, coinciding with the end of her marriage engagement. At 30 years old, she felt like her life was 'out of control' with both her personal and professional lives in chaos. Amy noticed that weeks seemed to just slip away and she was accomplishing very little. She

> *"Time is really the only capital that any human being has, and the only thing s/he cannot afford to lose."*
>
> —THOMAS EDISON

was seeing a therapist to work on her emotional and relationship issues, but she knew that she was spinning her wheels in her job search.

A friend suggested that Amy join a community employment network and, at the suggestion of the network facilitator, she immediately got to work on a daily schedule. She made a list of all her daily/weekly activities and plugged them into her plan, promising to report her activities at the end of each workday. She opted for a 5-day plan, giving herself Saturdays and Sundays off. Amy also made the wise decision to seek out a job-search buddy. She and her buddy committed to sending each other their completed daily plans by 8:00 p.m. each work night. In her first week, Amy said she had accomplished 60 percent of her plan, but by the third week she was completing 80-90 percent. Within four months, she had secured a new position.

Exercises: Daily Planning Tool

1. Make copies and complete your Daily Planning Tool. Customize it with other activities you identify to move you closer to a new job. For example, if there are specific web sites or trade publications that cater to your industry, be sure to include checking those sites and publications as part of your daily or weekly activities.

2. Think about who would make a good job-search buddy. A reciprocal relationship, where you each function as the other's job-search buddy, works well, but anyone you can rely on to hold you accountable to your plan is fine. Someone who was laid off with you is a strong choice, or perhaps a networking meeting contact. Just make sure you get along with this person reasonably well and that they are as serious about their job search as you are.

Write down the name(s) of potential candidates and discuss the idea with them. Identify one and develop a plan together to check in at least twice a week to share goals and progress toward these goals.

Indicate web sites and/or publications you plan to research.

_____
_____
_____

Potential job search buddies and their contact information:

_____
_____
_____

(Note: After completing all eight chapters of the book, you will probably have more activities to add to your planning sheets.)

STRATEGY #2

How Did I Get Here?

Good job seekers can tell you their industry, job history, degrees, and professional credentials. They can talk a bit about their last position and a little about the job they would like to get. In other words, they can summarize their resumés.

Great job seekers reflect carefully on their last position, what they've learned, and where they want to go next. They evaluate their successes and failures and their likes and dislikes, to help pinpoint the types of positions that will be the best fit for them and vice versa. They think through what skills and talents have contributed most to their accomplishments. They know what they have to offer and who is likely to value their skills, accomplishments and experiences, and they know how to present themselves in such a way that their professional attributes will be perceived as real and valuable.

Great job seekers can reach all the way back to the beginning of their careers and cite the milestones along the path that brought them to where they are today. They can talk about the college class that they took that really turned them on to anthropology, for example, or the professor that inspired them to go to grad school. They can tell you exactly what happened on the internship that led to the development of their thesis that helped them land their first job. They can explain how they met their future spouse at that position and about how they transferred to a new city where they joined a professional group as a membership volunteer and found out about their next position while doing volunteer work.

In essence, great job seekers know the road they've traveled and how they got to be where they are today. They are self-aware and self-confident.

Good job seekers say, I'm an accountant, I'm a secretary, I'm a doctor, or I'm a bookkeeper. When they're looking for work, they say that they need to find an opening for an accountant or a secretary or a doctor or a bookkeeper.

Great job seekers know that they're much more than a job title. They're in-touch with the driving forces that got them into that profession. A great job-seeking doctor says, "I've known since I was nine years old that I wanted to help people to heal. When my sister was sick with the measles, I did everything I could to make her feel better. I remember interviewing my pediatrician for a sixth grade assignment to do a report on a professional. As I wrote that report, I knew that's what I wanted to be when I grew up." You might not have had such a remarkable calling, but you probably selected your profession based on some very real reasons.

Describe your first thoughts of a career and what attracted your interest. What do you remember? Was it a discussion with an adult? Maybe your high-school guidance counselor? What was that discussion like? Or maybe you observed someone working in a profession that appealed to you. What skill sets or talents appealed to you as something you could either already do or would like to learn? What did you want to be when you grew up?

The Attorney: Ellen
Ellen knew she wanted to be a lawyer from age 10. She remembers standing on the steps of the Supreme Court during a family trip to Washington, DC, asking her parents what went on inside the building. They explained to her that the judges interpret the rules of law for the United States and that they are the highest court in the land.

She asked what you needed to do to get there and they explained that typically you need to go to college first and then law school. She absorbed the information, processed it, and with a very satisfied look on her face, announced she now knew what she was going to be when she grew up—she decided she was headed for law school. Yes, she had some bumps along the way, like when Sandra Day O'Connor became the first woman supreme court judge, as she thought she'd be first, but to this day she traces her career decision back to her exposure to the supreme court as a 10-year-old.

> "He who knows others is wise. He who knows himself is enlightened."
>
> —LAO TZU

The Kid Who Could Draw: Dan

"I was always the kid who could draw. Whenever anyone got stuck on their art project they asked me to help. That's what I always was: "the artist." Whenever I had free time, I drew and painted. It was just what came naturally to me. I always looked forward to art class. I remember when my friend's dad came to our Industrial Arts class and showed us his work as an Industrial Designer. I saw his product drawings and thought they were the coolest things in the world. After his presentation was over I approached him to learn more. He showed me his entire portfolio and invited me to visit his design studio at a large corporation. Of course I jumped at the chance. I knew that was what I'd want to do when I grew up!"

Dan was lucky to have a very specific talent and interest from an early age, but everyone has a path that leads to today's career choice. It could be happenstance, e.g., your friend's company had an opening for an entry-level buyer; you thought you'd give it a try and 10 years later it's still your field. But there were reasons you stayed with it. It's important to dig a little to discover more about your personal talents and skills and how you developed them. And it's also important to understand why other fields didn't work out.

The self-reflective individual who talks about his or her path and notable milestones is far more impressive to interviewers than someone who spouts "resumé talk." This demonstrates maturity and an understanding of how specific personal background elements are relevant to the job in question. These are valuable traits for many jobs. It's also good for you to understand your own path so you can make wiser decisions about the kind of work environment, people, and culture that are likely to work well for you.

The Family Business: Pete
Pete came from a family of engineers. His grandfather, father and three uncles were all electrical engineers, and he just assumed that's what he would be, too. So when Pete started failing his engineering classes at college he panicked. He couldn't believe he wasn't going to be successful in the field that his family had always prospered in. Happily, Pete had enough confidence to realize that he was enjoying his English and Economics classes and was advised to look into those areas as potential professions. After graduating from college as an English major, he got a job in a corporate marketing department. He loved the work and ended up taking more business classes in the evening and earning an MBA. The last time we spoke, he was working as a manager at a large business management consulting firm.

Exercise: Milestones—How You Got to Be In the Field You Are In Today

1. Think back on your childhood experiences, your education, and your career. Reflect on the major milestones of your life that made you who you are today in a professional sense. If possible, use a big sheet of butcher block paper, or you can also use two ordinary sheets of 8 ½" x 11" paper, taped together in landscape format. Draw a long horizontal line. Mark your key milestone activities and their dates: key childhood experiences/exposures, high school accomplishments, jobs and/or areas of interest, your first job and what you learned about yourself from it, college or special training and what you accomplished/learned about yourself from that. Mark down any other special training and other jobs to generate a long view of yourself as a professional.

_____
_____
_____
_____

2. Take a break and do another activity for at least 15 minutes. Think once again about your career and the things that influenced you along the way. Return to the Milestone Chart and re-work, revise, edit, change anything. Make sure this trajectory truly reflects your understanding of your career development.

_____
_____
_____
_____

STRATEGY #3

Your Career Story

Good job seekers know their employment history and can talk about each job on their resumé, but they have not yet strategically positioned themselves with a compelling story that puts them in a positive light.

Great job seekers take the time to prepare their "Career Profile" or "Corporate Story" before committing to a resumé. They position themselves for success in a fresh, unique, compelling way. They know how to communicate the stepping stones of their careers, including transitions and bumps in the road, in a way that positions them as self-aware individuals making wise judgments and decisions, and gaining skills and insights along the way.

I've had many clients describe their work history, and with certain jobs their body language tells me they have shame and embarrassment. Eliminate the stories you don't feel good about, or find a way to talk about the lessons you learned and how you emerged wiser, more compassionate, more cautious, or other positive learning you were able to take from the situation.

Responsible Father: Mike

One of my clients, "Mike," had to take seven months off to help his teenage daughter with serious psychological issues. A nasty divorce was at the root of the problem, and Mike's daughter took the brunt of it. He had no choice but to be there for her. Mike's company wouldn't give him an extended leave, so he quit his job and took a sabbatical so he could be there for his daughter. Now he was worried about explaining the gap in his resumé.

Mike devised an honest, heartfelt story about living his values, how much he learned about himself during this period, and, most impor-

> "The definition of insanity is to keep doing the same things and expect a different outcome."
>
> —ALBERT EINSTEIN

tantly, how his daughter came through it all, healed and ready to move on with her life. What employer wouldn't be impressed with this story? On his resumé he describes the gap as, "Medical Sabbatical," and in person he tells the full story.

"I actually welcome the chance to explain my seven-month gap now because it reminds me of the strength of my own values. It took a lot of courage for me to risk leaving work for a whole year, but I knew then and I still feel now that it was the right thing to do. I always emphasize that I'm a responsible parent by mentioning that I made sure I had enough money to support my family for the year I gave myself to take care of my daughter."

"I'm proud when I tell the story. Sometimes I wonder how I'd feel about it if my daughter hadn't improved, but fortunately she did improve, and I feel good about the fact that I put my values into action. I think employers are impressed with that kind of integrity as well. Otherwise, they're probably not the right company for me, anyway."

If you overcame a difficult personal situation, create a story and practice telling it. Don't apologize for it; own it, and make it interesting. It's your story and it needs to make sense to you before you use it on prospective employers.

Know thyself in a career sense. You must clarify and be able to articulate today's career profile, yesterday's history, and tomorrow's journey, and you must be able to convey to employers how and why you fit into their future.

Exercise: Create Your Story

1. Put your milestones from the last exercise into narrative form. Practice telling the story of your career choices and career development. Include specifics to make the story memorable and unique to you. For each milestone, what did you learn about yourself and how did that change your subsequent career/education/life choices moving forward?

_____
_____
_____
_____
_____
_____
_____

2. Develop and practice sharp anecdotes that enliven your work history and or credentials. In other words, breathe life into the words on your resumé. Be prepared to talk about your resumé in an interesting way. Transfer some of the enthusiasm to examples of how you'd demonstrate those characteristics, skills, and talents to the company you're applying to work for.

_____
_____
_____
_____
_____
_____
_____

3. Look at any gaps in your resumé. Tell the story of what happened. If it's a period you feel ashamed of, think about what you learned from the experience.

4. Find two or three people to tell your story to. Ask for honest and specific feedback on how you come across. Specifically, ask them at which points you come across as strong and confident and which ones, if any, you come across as weak or ashamed. Work on those parts of your story until you can tell them in a more positive light.

5. Describe your perfect job. What skills and talents does it require? What kind of people do you work with? What is the management style? What is the corporate culture and values? Communicate this to a colleague or job search buddy and ask them if it sounds well thought out, compelling, interesting, realistic, and congruent with how they see you.

STRATEGY #4

The Emotional Roller Coaster

Good job seekers dread the emotional roller coaster of the job search process and fail to prepare adequately for it. They experience the ups and downs of the job search, going from hope and elation to disappointment and despair over and over with each new potential job.

Great job seekers prepare for the roller coaster, using rational practices to smooth out the ride. One vital skill possessed by successful job seekers is the ability to take one's own "emotional temperature."

It's important to know when your frustration and stress levels reach the point at which you cannot interview effectively. You can't be an effective job seeker when you're stressed, fatigued, and frustrated, so when you feel these effectiveness killers coming on, it's time to recharge. Tune in. Look at yourself in the mirror and practice talking about your job skills. You'll know when it's time for a break. If not, check in with a family member or friend. Then, do what it takes to recharge your batteries.

For minor burnout, take a walk or a drive, or go for a coffee with your job search buddy. In some cases, you may need a longer break. Get some exercise. Go hiking or biking or running. Go to the movies. Take the afternoon off and go to the beach or the woods.

Nature is especially good at helping us get centered and relaxed. Review your confidence cards (see page 34 where you will create your confidence cards. Do some deep breathing. Look at old picture albums that make you happy. Listen to music. Dance. Do whatever restores your sense of wellbeing so you can project yourself in a positive way.

It's normal to have strong positive and negative emotions during your job search. Employment is about survival. It determines in a very direct way the kind of life you'll lead, and that makes employment one of the most serious aspects of a person's life. So it makes sense that a job search can evoke tremendous highs, terrible lows, and everything in between. We need to anticipate these states and build in ways to cope.

One common mistake job seekers make is falling in love with a job before it's theirs. I've had countless clients come to sessions very excited at having found a job opening that fits them to a tee. The company sounds great, and the job practically "has their name written on it." Here's the problem: this dream job probably sounds perfect to hundreds of other applicants as well.

Companies often hire marketing professionals just to write up these terrific-sounding job descriptions. They can make even a relatively mundane job sound like the most exciting thing ever. There's no way of knowing whether any given job is really what they say it is until you actually get the job. Even then, it takes time to know whether it's a good fit.

Think about it: You'd never agree to marry a person you'd never met in person, even if that person sounded ideal. Falling in love with a job description is the equivalent of getting engaged to someone before you even meet them.

On some level, we're all optimists, hoping for that perfect job. It's great to have hope, but it's even better to apply a healthy amount of caution during your job search. You need to use clear judgment and critical thinking because the job search process may take longer than you expected, and we need to keep ourselves strong and healthy on all levels: emotionally, physically, mentally, and spiritually. I received an email recently from a client who included a "fabulous" job description and how she felt that this was the one. I had to tell her that she could very well be setting herself up for disappointment.

FACT: Many of the jobs listed online are stale. Many job listings have already been filled, and yet companies keep them running anyway to collect resumés for their files. This way they don't have to pay recruiters and headhunters if they need to fill additional jobs later on.

Do Not Fall in Love with a Job Until it is Yours

So repeat after me: "I will not fall in love with a company or with a job until it's mine and until I've had time to be on the job and determine the fit." This is also good advice because many verbal offers

"When you get into a tight place and it seems you can't go on, hold on, for that's just the place and the time that the tide will turn."

—HARRIET BEECHER STOWE

never reach the final stage. A job is not real until you have shown up and actually begun the job!

Stressed Out: Barbara

Barbara was devastated when she lost her six-figure-salary position as a corporate events manager. After a year-long search, she was happy to find a $20-per-hour job with a neighbor's company. Unfortunately, she'd already lost her home and had to withdraw her daughter from an expensive private school.

Barbara had developed health problems from the tremendous stress she was under and realized she needed to do something to cope. She took up competitive swimming at a local pool and as her resilience improved she ended up finding a new, well paying job as a corporate events manager. In the process, she learned what all job seekers must learn—ways to cope with the emotional challenges of the job search process.

Take the lead from great job seekers who find many effective ways to cope with stress. Try building in rewards for positive developments—getting a call for a second interview, for example. Reward yourself with an hour just to read your favorite magazine, or call an old friend just to chat for an hour. Take a bubble bath. Drive out to a peaceful spot in nature where you go to think. Treat yourself to a delicious cappuccino. Rewards don't have to cost a lot of money; indeed, some of the best rewards—going for a hike, playing with your pet, reading for pleasure, for example—don't have to cost any money at all.

Similarly, when bad news comes along, make a special effort to make yourself feel better and restore your confidence. Great job seekers anticipate ups and downs and create ways to cope.

A Great Stress-buster

Robert, a member of our employment network, told me that after a few months of his job search he was dealing with a lot of fatigue and anxiety. Once he became aware of the problem, he developed a practice that has been very helpful, not only to him but to everyone in the employment network he's shared it with. He noticed that it was not only energizing, but that it changed his whole outlook.

Robert's Happiness Practice (Try it, it works!)

- Practice breathing in HAPPINESS and breathing out FEAR.

- Make them long, deep breaths.

- As you breathe in happiness, you can't help but smile, and as you breathe out fear you can't help but feel a sense of relief and an unburdening.

- You feel lighter and easier, and you can feel the tension leaving your system.

If you need a pep talk, call your job search buddy, or a friend or family member, someone who supports and respects you for all the positive things that you do and are. Someone who sees and respects all that you've accomplished. These are important people to have in your life, especially now, as you navigate the job search process. Great job seekers have at least one job search buddy, and many have two or three.

Exercise: Riding the Waves with Confidence

1. Make your own confidence cards!

Get a few pieces of cardboard or poster board and cut out 10-15 playing card-sized pieces.

Look at your resumé and think about your accomplishments. Think about the skills and traits each of those accomplishments represent. Then, on each card, write down one of those traits and add two or three examples of when you demonstrated that trait. Try to make at least 10 or MORE of these cards.

Put a rubber band around your pack of confidence cards and carry them around with you so you'll have easy access to them at all times.

Add to them as you develop new skills and capabilities.

Remember, no one can take away the truth of your confidence cards. Just look at the trait and turn it over to remind yourself of your real accomplishments. By using these cards, you'll see in black and white reality that you really do have some great qualities, and a track record of success to support those claims.

Indicate the traits you 'own' for your confidence cards.
Some examples: reliable, honest, good with numbers, communication skills, organizational skills, get along well with co-workers, flexible, meet deadlines, punctual, leadership skills, managerial skills, budget development, proposal writing, project management skills, editorial skills.

2. List at least five ways to reward yourself when the chips are down to help you smooth out the emotional roller coaster of the job-search process.

STRATEGY #5

Rallying Your Personal Network

More than 80 percent of available jobs are never posted or advertised; they're filled through personal connections. And that means how you use and expand your personal network is key in getting your next job.

Good job seekers mention to some of their friends, colleagues, relatives, and neighbors that they're looking for work. Sometimes they even do a follow up email with their resumé attached and hope for the best.

Great job seekers create a strategic communications vehicle directed at ALL of their friends, colleagues, neighbors, former managers, mentors, professors, dentists, doctors—anyone and everyone they can think of who knows them fairly well and wants to see them succeed. They update their list of contacts regularly and remind them clearly about their current situation, past accomplishments, and exactly the kind of work they're looking for.

Great job seekers ask for leads, ideas, connections, job openings, and suggestions. They encourage everyone in their network to keep up with them on both personal and professional topics. This type of communication is more personal in tone than a cover letter to a stranger, but it provides key information that makes it easy for people to help you in your job search.

You'll want to send out an updated version of this letter regularly, maybe quarterly or even monthly. Don't let too much time go by, and DO update the group once you've landed a job (See Strategy #8 about follow up once you've secured your new position).

Below are two examples of "friends and family letters," each with a different tone and personality. You're asking for their help, so take some time to establish the appropriate format, approach, and tone. I changed some details to protect the individuals' identity. And yes, there is room for (appropriate and timely) humor, as you'll see in Andy's letter.

Example #1: Shannon Called it Her "Friends and Family Letter"

Hi <First Name>,

I hope this note finds you doing well. I continue to search for that next great employment opportunity, which is the reason that I'm writing you. You may recall that last summer my position at Pharm-Gene was eliminated.

Since that time I've reconnected with many wonderful friends and colleagues, and with their help in raising my resumé's visibility I have had the good fortune to be considered for a few positions with some great companies. However, given the current economic environment and the sheer numbers of qualified candidates seeking employment, I have yet to land that next job.

I'm contacting you today to recruit you to join the "Find Shannon a Job!" campaign.

How Can You Help?
Participation requires just a small amount of time. Below is a brief description of the kind of work I'm looking for and the type of companies that would be looking for someone like me. However, knowing about specific job openings in my field is not required. I've also includ-

ed a list of companies that I am targeting in all of the areas where I'm conducting my job search: here in the San Francisco Bay Area as well as in the NYC area and Chicago.

- Do you know anyone at any of these companies?
- Would you be willing to put me in touch with them?

With so many jobs snagged through personal connections, the more people I get to know, the better my chances!

Please take a few moments to review the lists and information below and let me know if something sparks any ideas that might help me further my job search. I've attached a copy of my resumé so that you can forward it to any appropriate contacts you may have. The details of my job history also can be found in my LinkedIn profile at http://www.linkedin.com/in/shannonjohnston.

Thanks in advance for any assistance you can provide. I look forward to hearing from you, and of course I'm also interested in how you're doing. If there's anything I can do for you, please don't hesitate.

Thanks!

Best regards,
Shannon

(Listing of 25 companies)

Example #2: Andy Called it His "Economic Stimulus Plan"

Hi,

This may be unconventional but the economy is, too.

I've read that, in many cases, the people left behind in a company after a layoff have more stress than those let go. I can't speak for everyone who's currently not working, but I have to admit I've been enjoying our beautiful Bay Area weather—biking and completing many of those nagging home projects. Unfortunately, lottery tickets and that "penny stock" that just couldn't miss haven't panned out, so it is time to rejoin the work force.

I just completed a consulting project with _____ Corporation, implementing a new data center in Northern Virginia. I was the onsite network diagnostic person for the past 11 months, resolving network access issues as systems were transferred from existing data centers.

Now it's time to explore new opportunities in the San Francisco Bay Area, so I'm asking for your help. Having worked in both startups and large corporations, I've learned that it's the daily job challenges and co-workers that make the position exciting.

If you know of an interesting opportunity, or have a contact in an organization that you could put me in touch with, I would really appreciate it. I'm open to a variety of possibilities including senior-level project management, network infrastructure planning/design, and product management. Below is my LinkedIn profile URL, which includes details of my job history:

http://www.linkedin.com/in/andy

And of course, while my job search is important, just as important is the opportunity to reconnect with friends and former co-workers. So regardless of whether you know of any opportunities, please drop me a note when it's convenient to let me know how you're doing and what's new in your life.

I look forward to hearing from you.

Thanks,
Andy S.
Cell (650) 533-XXXX

Clients who've used this "friends and family letter" typically get at least 3-5 solid meetings/opportunities—not necessarily job offers, but good, solid, actionable leads. Plus, it strengthens relationships, which is crucial to long-term career success.

Some people send their letter by email, the advantage being that you can send many out, quickly (and cheaply), and you get quick responses, too. One of my clients sent out 92 emails and received seven responses within the first three hours, one of which was a direct job lead. Within 36 hours she had 20 responses and had secured two job interviews! I cannot understate the importance of identifying and leveraging your personal network community.

Despite the advantages of email, I suggest that you use good old snail-mail to send out these letters. Several clients reported to me that many of their recipients never received the email note because it went to their SPAM folders. You don't want to risk missing vital members of your circle. Plus, nobody gets much personal mail anymore, and your handwritten envelope makes it a special, personal communication. It'll be more likely to be read and taken seriously.

> *"Alone we can do so little; together we can do so much."*
>
> —HELEN KELLER

I've had clients do it both ways, and snail-mail generates better results. You could even send your note both ways and tell your recipients that you wanted to make sure it reached them.

I also suggest a follow-up call to each person within a week of mailing or emailing them. Follow up at least once every three months until you get a job. Then (per Strategy #8), once you land your next job, send them a letter to tell them about your new job, thank them for their help, and to offer to return the favor.

**Exercise:
Your Economic Stimulus Plan or Friends and Family Letter**

1. Compile a list of names and contact info (email or snail-mail addresses) for everyone on your list. Include friends, colleagues, neighbors, relatives, former managers, professors, mentors, and anyone else you can think of.

_____
_____
_____
_____
_____
_____
_____
_____
_____
_____

2. Draft your first letter. Don't forget to proofread it before sending it out. If you're using email, make sure everyone receives a "blind copy" so that people only see their own address. Be sure to include the following:

- A brief, friendly salutation
- An update on your transition
- What you're looking for
- Your key skills/accomplishments that you can contribute
- A request for leads, intros, connections, conferences, ideas, etc.
- Ask how you might be of assistance to them
- Mention that you will follow up again in 2 weeks, 1 month, 2 months

Have someone other than you proofread the letter yet once again, before you send it out. We often miss our own mistakes!

Follow up as promised. In fact, call 10 of the recipients for more personal follow up and perhaps to get some quick leads, ideas, introductions, or connections.

3. Develop 2-3 follow up questions to use during conversations with people on your friends and family list. For example, you could ask them which social media sites they use and how they use them. You can ask how they got their current job and how their company typically hires people.

Now develop your own questions:

_____
_____
_____
_____
_____
_____
_____
_____
_____
_____
_____
_____
_____
_____
_____

STRATEGY #6

The Interview is YOUR Audition

Good job seekers view an interview as an INTERVIEW. They prepare for an interview by anticipating how to respond to the interviewer's agenda; they use a reactive preparation style. They assume that the interviewer has all the control. They typically have prepared responses to the generic (yet important) questions about strengths and weaknesses, past job experiences, reasons for leaving, and questions about technical aspects of the job requirements and qualifications.

Great job seekers view an interview as an AUDITION—an opportunity to showcase their best selves. They prepare not only by anticipating and practicing answering questions from the interviewer, but also by creating their own agenda. They use a proactive preparation style. They're ready to shape the agenda, not just respond to it.

Great job seekers are well versed in their own strengths and weaknesses, key achievements, professional skills, and capabilities, and they have also thoroughly researched the company and its bigger picture needs and situation.

Great job seekers know the vital importance of establishing strong rapport with the interviewer. Without a strong connection, influence and persuasion are nearly impossible. It's vital that you learn how to build strong rapport—how to get on the same wavelength as your interviewer to ensure that you'll create a positive impression. Fortunately, there are research-backed techniques that you can employ here.

Great job seekers always ask an interviewer, "What are the key traits and skills needed to be successful in this position? And they are always prepared to clearly articulate how their qualifica-

tions fulfill (at least some of) those requirements. Because great job seekers know their professional story backwards and forwards and know how to best position their background.

An excellent technique for creating quick rapport with a person is called MIRRORING, and it means exactly what the word implies. Imagine watching yourself in the mirror. When you move, the image in the mirror moves. When you're still, it's still. It moves at the same pace as you do, etc. Watch the way the interviewer sits and moves, and mimic those movements, not in an obvious way, but so that you're matching their energy level and posture.

Mirroring is verbal, too. When you meet your interviewer, behave as he or she does. If they speak quickly, you speak quickly. If they speak softly, you speak softly. Eye contact is vital. Don't stare; appropriate eye contact uses "gentle eyes." Practice this skill with a family member or friend. You may want to find out how the people at that organization dress, and either dress the way they do, or maybe move it up a notch to show respect.

Mirroring is an easily learned skill. Unconsciously, people feel warm and positive toward those who are like them. By mirroring their behavior, you create rapport. You might also want to look into a more detailed approach to creating rapport, called neurolinguistic programming (NLP). You can look it up online to learn more.

Great job seekers craft statements about how they can help the company solve its problems and achieve greater success. They can answer questions, but they also know how to extend it to include information they know will be helpful in communicating their qualifications relative to the specific needs of the position, the hiring manager, and/or the company.

This is what great politicians do. If you listen carefully to a politician during a campaign interview, no matter what the question, they always manage to get their agenda across. This is a very effective communication strategy to employ during interviews, too.

Remember, your interviewer is listening not only to the content of what you're saying, but also the TONE of your responses. Typically interviewers like to see the following traits:

- Enthusiasm
- Articulateness
- Self awareness
- Competence
- Good vocabulary
- Good listening skills
- Reflective and thoughtful

Paul Does a 360 with His Interview Skills

Paul felt defeated by the interview he had recently been on, prompting him to seek professional assistance. He had researched the company, developed a long list of thoughtful questions and gone into the interview feeling excited and ready. An hour later he came out disappointed and frustrated. Yes, he had a chance to ask all of his questions and he had listened well and gained tremendous knowledge of the company and the specific job requirements. However, Paul never communicated his unique background, qualifications and demonstrated skills to show that he would be the premier choice. He was excluded from the next round of interviews, and that's when he came to me. Afterward, his approach was completely different, and he ended up landing a job and felt that his improved interviewing (auditioning) and mirroring skills contributed significantly to his success.

Note: Mirroring is also an excellent technique to use once you land your new job. Match your pacing, eye contact, and overall style to that of your new colleagues and you will increase the likelihood of starting off on the right foot to build strong working relationships.

"It sometimes seems that intense desire creates not only its own opportunities, but its own talents."

—ERIC HOFFER

Exercise: Crafting Your Political Campaign

1. Find a real job opening, job title, and job description for a position you would like to be interviewed for.

2. Research the company and learn about their problems, needs, situation, and environment. If possible, using LinkedIn or other networking tools. Find some people who work at that company and ask them about its current needs, culture, and problems. Ask specifics about the position (if possible) and anything that might help you prepare a relevant, powerful agenda for your "audition."

3. Prepare a list of your 3-5 key skills, accomplishments, talents, and credentials—capabilities that you know are relevant to filling out the job beautifully. Practice articulating ALL of them and PRACTICE inserting that information into a discussion.

You can always take advantage of the part of the interview when you're asked if you have any questions. Answer that with, "I do have information that I'd like to share with you that I believe you'll find relevant and helpful in getting to know me and my fit for your position." Then continue with your key 3-5 succinct, well-articulated statements.

_____
_____
_____
_____
_____
_____

4. Practice MIRRORING. You can practice it with anyone, even a good friend or family member. Watch them closely and do as they do. See if they notice a change in you. Ask how they feel about you after you've consciously mirrored them during a discussion. When you feel you've "got it," use your new skill at your next interview!

STRATEGY #7

To Join or Not to Join—Professional Associations and Social Media

Good job seekers join relevant professional organizations and alumni associations. They might even attend meetings, but they either don't talk to anyone or they talk to just one or two people who are inconsequential to their job search. They browse through job listings and read online job forums. They may even subscribe to group publications and attend networking meetings, often finding the professional associations to be a waste of time and money.

Great job seekers are strategic in their selection of and involvement with professional associations. They research and find the ones that are often NOT attended by their competition. For example, smart marketing professionals who are targeting high-tech companies avoid marketing groups. Yes, they may read up on their industry, but they join groups targeted to the high-tech industry that industry leaders might attend.

Great job seekers look for the leaders of the professional associations they're interested in. They call the leader, introduce themselves as a potential member and ask which events they recommend. Great job seekers ask if they might meet personally with that leader and get introductions to folks who might be good for their job search efforts.

Great job seekers call the Membership Chair, the person who knows who's who and is interested in attracting new members. Again, great job seekers introduce themselves and ask about specific kinds of people with job titles and interests who would be valuable to meet. They might even have some companies in mind and ask if the group has any members who are employees

As of April 2010 more than 60 million people joined LinkedIN. They developed their profiles and are making professional connections. Recruiters rely on LInkedIN. As a great job seeker, you will be there, too!

of those companies. They VOLUNTEER to assist the Membership Director or the Program Chair. These are two VERY visible activities.

After completing my Master's degree in Instructional Technology, I began my first professional job as a training development specialist. At my graduate school advisor's suggestion, I not only joined a professional training association, I also sought a leadership role for continued career advancement. I began to assist the Program Chair, and when his tenure was complete, I took over. Through that role, I met with anyone and everyone I wanted, for the sake of arranging programs. I ended up getting to know some top Stanford University professors who proved to be very influential in my career. I was also exposed to top managers at a company I had targeted to join, Apple Computer. In that role I met a future colleague at a company who recommended me!

Good job seekers immerse themselves in social media. Unfortunately, many of them get so immersed online, they practically drown in it! That said, social media and online job boards and the rest of the online world contain vital tools for the job search, but they can also have a dangerous undertow, pulling you out to a vast online sea, where you can easily get lost.

The social media world changes rapidly. As of mid-2010, the most popular professional social media site is LinkedIn, and many people are also using Facebook and Twitter in their job searches. My best recommendation on this is to find out which sites your colleagues are using and how they are using them, and limit and structure your time on them. If you do chose to have a presence, make sure it's honest, professional and up-to-date. Remember to treat everything you put online as if it will be there forever.

Most of us have an online footprint whether we know it or not. Do online searches of your name to see what comes up. If you decide to start a blog, be sure to include only information, opinions, and ideas that you'd be pleased to have any potential employer see.

My observation is that great job seekers spend a lot of time in DIRECT contact with people building relationships that will lead to their next job. They plant seeds online, too, but they concentrate on live, face-to-face meetings and interactions wherever they can. In person meetings are what will get you hired, not surfing the Internet.

Research commissioned by Microsoft in December 2009 found that 79% of U.S. hiring managers and job recruiters surveyed reviewed online information about job applicants.

Exercise: You Can Connect!

1. Research some professional associations and/or alumni groups. List them here.

_____
_____
_____
_____
_____
_____
_____
_____
_____
_____
_____

Narrow your search to 2-3 groups and review their web sites, past events, blogs, and other elements.

Contact at least two of each group's leaders—the Membership Chair and the Program Chair, for example.

Ask questions such as:

- Do you have members from XYZ company/organization?
- Would you introduce me to them at the next event?
- I am seeking a position as [job title]. Do many people in that role attend your meetings?
- Do you maintain a forum for job listings?
- Here are some of my skills and interests. How can I contribute to your organization?

2. Social Media—Ask five colleagues about their use of social media.

Ask them not only what sites they consider vital in their industry but how much time they spend on each one. Ask them about online job boards and which ones they feel include the best, most up-to-date listings. Ask for any tips they have on using the sites.

STRATEGY #8

Landing the Job

Good job seekers breathe a deep sigh of relief when they finally land a new job. They throw away their job-search binders, and thank their lucky stars that their job-search days are over.

Great job seekers give themselves a chance to celebrate and enjoy their success. Then they take a deep breath, turn the page in their job search binders, and enter a new chapter title with the name of their new position and the new company or organization. They remind themselves that they'll continue adding new accomplishments, skills, and experiences.

Great job seekers update their friends, colleagues, and recruiters with info about their new position. They update their LinkedIn profile and any other online resumés and professional profiles. They keep updating their online profiles with new achievements, accomplishments, and any training and development programs and skills.

I highly recommend that you send personal thank you notes to those who were particularly helpful to your job search. You may even want to consider taking some special people to lunch. These might include close family members and friends who helped you though the ups and downs of your job search.

Great job seekers keep in contact with their circle of influencers at least quarterly. They stay in the mind's eye of their influence circle and continually work on expanding it. They keep playing visible roles in their professional organizations and alumni groups and even try to get their new company to pay for such memberships.

Great job seekers recognize that the world of employment moves quickly and that even though they may have a great job now, things happen. So they sort their CONFIDENCE CARDS and keep them nearby, hopeful and confident but always vigilantly tuned in and ready for yet another round as a GREAT JOB SEEKER.

Surprise Success Story!—Andy, Who Wrote the Economic Stimulus Letter in Chapter 5

On Monday, April 19th, 2010 Andy began his new job as a Project Manager. He found his job through a former manager from 15 years back whom he had contacted via LinkedIn. Andy was smart not to have burned any bridges!

Q&A with Andy:

1. In retrospect, which job seeking activities were the most and least worthwhile?
The best were communications with friends and acquaintances including the Employment Network meetings which kept up my spirits. Taking care of my physical and mental health—exercise and companionship helps. My dogs got a lot of exercise! Least productive was sending resumes to companies through job posting web sites and culling through web site job listings.

2. What surprises and or challenges come to mind?
Keeping a positive attitude—making sure your finances are in shape. A surprise was how little free time I had even though I was unemployed. Forty hours can get filled quickly.

3. Thoughts on how to best ride the emotional roller coaster of the process?

Don't isolate yourself—get out of the house, get together with friends—join a job seeking group, go to association meetings in your field. Realize you can't be in control of everything and the reasons you might be interviewed/hired are not all based on what you said or didn't say. Know that some days you might feel depressed—it will pass.

4. How do you respond when friends and neighbors ask how it's going?

Don't give in to negativity—I wasn't in this situation because I was a bad person or a lousy worker. Many people have been between jobs for one reason or another. Look for positive things to come out of the conversation—a possible job lead, a chance to get together for coffee, a work contact or just let people know how you are feeling—good or bad. Trust your instincts and don't worry about what others think.

5. What are you doing differently, if anything, in your new job in light of your experience with a tough unemployment period?

For now I think it is important to understand the interpersonal and political relationships in my company. I also want to stay relevant and get professional certifications. And I plan to network more with friends and business acquaintances—you never know!

6. Are you doing follow up to all who helped you along the way?

Yes—I sent it an update email to everyone I had been in contact with, and I personally called a few of the people who were in my close circle. I also updated my LinkedIn which sent an update to a much larger audience than my personal email.

> *"And will you succeed? Yes indeed, yes indeed! Ninety-eight and three-quarters percent guaranteed!"*
>
> —DR. SEUSS

Exercise: Still Some Work to Do

1. List all the people you need to call personally to announce your new job and new contact info. Place an asterisk next to the names of those who need to be sent a personal thank you note.

_____
_____
_____
_____
_____

2. List all the people you need to email with your updates. Include recruiters, job coaches, networking partners, informational interviewers, etc.

_____
_____
_____
_____
_____

3. List all of the online career profile sites you need to update.

_____
_____
_____
_____

4. Plan on a quarterly resumé/profile update. Indicate the dates over the next two years when you will make those updates. Enter the dates into your calendar.

_____
_____
_____
_____
_____

5. Again, use the MIRRORING technique (as described in Strategy #6 of this book) with your new co-workers. People respond well to newcomers on a team who are similar to them. They tend to have higher levels of trust and comfort with people who have a similar style, pacing and overall way of being. Of course, be yourself too, but be finely tuned to the prevailing culture. Your initial positive impression will make a strong foundation on which you can build solid working relationships in your new organization. Onward to your success!

About Joan

Originally from New York, Joan has been in Silicon Valley since 1983, arriving with a Master's Degree in Instructional Technology (training) to develop sales training for Memorex Corporation. Several award winning programs later she was recruited by Apple Computer to design training to launch the Macintosh computer to business and government channels. She succeeded and was promoted into marketing with user group programs becoming her specialty. During her time at Apple, Joan was asked to build and deliver an Informational Interviewing course at The Career Action Center. That class led to many more, and began her ongoing involvement and passion for career training and career coaching. Four years into her Apple stint Joan was recruited to 3Com Corporation to spearhead a global user group program and in her four years at the company, initiated a total of seven global programs, leading a team of 8 people.

After ten years of corporate management, Joan launched Focused Marketing, a consultancy providing full service marketing and communications to both large companies like Intel, Tandem and Fujitsu and start-ups including Com21, Xpedion, NetBuy and Luminate. Later, in the 90s, Joan married and built a family with her husband, David. When the economy took a dive, she devoted her energies to building employment networks to help people get back to work and re-started career coaching. It was during that time that she came up with the idea for Greatin8Coaching.com books, using the best of learning technologies to create a short, fast, interactive way for people to quickly gain skills in new areas. Stay tuned for continued titles in the Greatin8Coaching books series. And feel free to contact Joan with new programs and projects.

joan@Greatin8Coaching.com

Author Appreciation

Thank you to the magical designer, Lauren Smith who has been exceeding my expectations for more than 20 years. Lauren immediately 'got' my vision for the Greatin8Coaching.com series and visually created it; equal in beauty and functionality.

A big thank you to my best friend of 30+ years, Susan Woog Wagner, photographer extraordinaire, for the lovely picture she took of me for this book. Thank you Arleen Reetz, a talented communication professional who provided editorial skills and vital encouragement.

Thank you to all the people at Peninsula Temple Beth El for working with me to create the Employment Network. I am proud to be a part of such a wonderfully caring community. I'd like to especially thank: Rabbi Dennis Eisner, Lolli Freedman, Colleen Devlin, Phil Abrams and Rick Kadet.

I want to acknowledge the support of Sid Jacobson, a well known author who has shown tremendous support for Greatin8Coaching.com book series. I also appreciate Lisa Ann Pinkerton and Joe Guiterez, talented PR folks, who are showing tremendous enthusiasm and looking to generate widespread attention for Greatin8Coaching.com book series!

And much gratitude to all of the hardworking and dedicated career coaching clients I've had the pleasure to work with, and guide on their employment journey.

And from the heart, much gratitude always to my sweet husband David and precious son, Daniel. You add joy to my life each and

Notes

www.ingramcontent.com/pod-product-compliance
Lightning Source LLC
LaVergne TN
LVHW071651060526
838200LV00029B/422